Chris Zorich

by Mark Stewart

ACKNOWLEDGMENTS

The editors wish to thank Chris Zorich for his cooperation in preparing this book. Thanks also to Zorich Industries for their assistance.

PHOTO CREDITS

All photos courtesy AP/Wide World Photos except the following:

Olympia Dukakis – 37
Rob Tringali, Jr./Sports Chrome – Cover, 23 top, 24, 30, 31, 32
University of Notre Dame – 16, 24 right
Chris Zorich – 8, 9, 14, 15, 40 top
The Chris Zorich Foundation – 12, 34, 35, 43

STAFF

Project Coordinator: John Sammis, Cronopio Publishing
Series Design Concept: The Sloan Group
Design and Electronic Page Makeup: Jaffe Enterprises, and
          Digital Communications Services, Inc.

LIBRARY OF CONGRESS CATALOGING-IN-PUBLICATION DATA

Stewart, Mark.
    Chris Zorich / by Mark Stewart.
        p. cm. – (Grolier all-pro biographies)
    Includes index.
    Summary: A brief biography of the all-pro defender for the Chicago Bears.
    ISBN 0-516-20140-9 (lib. binding)–ISBN 0-516-26002-2 (pbk.)
    1. Zorich, Chris, 1969-   –Juvenile literature. 2. Football players–United States–Biography–
Juvenile literature. [1. Zorich, Chris, 1969-   . 2. Football players.] I. Title. II. Series.
GV939.Z665S84 1996
796.332'092–dc20
[B]   96-33794
                                                                                          CIP
                                                                                          AC

The Grolier All-Pro Biographies™ are produced in cooperation with
    Sports Media, Incorporated, New York, NY.

Grolier ALL-PRO Biographies™

Chris Zorich

by
Mark Stewart

CHILDREN'S PRESS®
A Division of Grolier Publishing
New York • London • Hong Kong • Sydney
Danbury, Connecticut

Contents

Who

Am I?

When I hear people say how tough and dangerous it is to be a professional football player, sometimes I have to smile. Yes, it is a very demanding job. And yes, there is always a chance you could be badly injured. But where I grew up, tough meant not having enough clothes to wear or enough food to eat. And danger lurked on every street corner and down every hallway. I made it out of that environment because I wanted something better for myself and my family. My name is Chris Zorich, and this is my story . . . "

#97

"I set my goals and went after them with everything I had."

Growing Up

Chris when he was one year old

L ife does not get much tougher for a kid than it was for Chris Zorich. He and his mother lived in a small apartment in one of the most dangerous sections of the city of Chicago. She suffered from diabetes, and had trouble finding work. They did their best to live on the $250 public assistance check that arrived in the mail each month. There was not much to smile about in Chris's neighborhood. Abandoned cars littered the streets and the vacant lot next to their building was a hang-out for drug dealers and gang members. Chris did not even feel safe in his own apartment—thieves broke in and stole everything they had five different times.

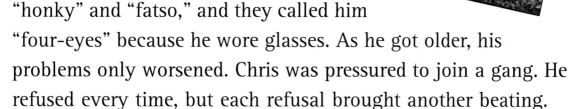

Chris's mom, Zora, came from a family that had once lived in Eastern Europe. His father was an African-American who left Zora before Chris was born. Because Chris was part black and part white he was a target for racial taunts and violence. He once estimated that he was beaten up more than 100 times by other children. They teased him with cruel names like "honky" and "fatso," and they called him "four-eyes" because he wore glasses. As he got older, his problems only worsened. Chris was pressured to join a gang. He refused every time, but each refusal brought another beating.

Chris liked to play sports because it took his mind off his problems. He started playing tackle football with his friends. They had no protective equipment and played right in the street, but it was still safer than walking through the neighborhood after sundown. When Chris told his mother he wanted to play in high school, she refused. Football, she said, was too dangerous.

No matter how much Chris begged her, she would not sign the consent form. Then Chris did a very bad thing. He signed his mom's name on the form and joined the team. When Zora found out, she was very angry. But the season had already begun and Chris had proved to be one of Chicago Vocational High School's best players. If he quit, he explained, he would let his friends down. Zora decided to let him play.

John Potocki was the team's coach. He saw that Chris was different than the other kids. After being beaten up and taunted for so many years, Chris had built up a lot of hate. Coach Potocki showed Chris how to get rid of all that anger through training hard and playing tough. He became so good at football that college recruiters began taking notice.

Chris began to realize that he had a chance to build a better life for himself and his mother. When he started playing football, he had never heard of a scholarship. Now many schools were offering him a chance to get a free college education in exchange for playing football. When Chris received a scholarship offer from Notre Dame University in South Bend, Indiana, he accepted.

"I didn't have any brothers or sisters. There was only me and my mom. She was a very loving person and she supported

In the neighborhood where Chris grew up, tunnels were dangerous places where drugs were sold, and where crime took place almost every day.

me 100 percent with everything I did. She's the person who taught me how to play baseball and football. She was always there for me, so I had a lot of love and care.

When I was a young kid, the gang bangers and the guys who sold drugs were my role models. I wanted to have a nice car and nice clothes and a lot of people hanging around me when I grew up. These guys seemed to have all that. I would do bad things like take candy without paying for it. And once, I threw a brick through the window of a police car. Fortunately, my mom explained to me that these things I was doing were

wrong. And she told me that I should not look up to people who sold drugs or joined gangs. I knew she was telling me the truth. From that day on, they were no longer my role models.

"My mom taught me to do the best I can possibly do at everything I do," Chris remembers. During junior high and high school, he helped Zora by taking a job as a janitor at the nearby Tabor Lutheran Church. "If I looked at the church floor and I had not mopped it well, I'd do it again.

"When I was a kid, I had a stuttering problem. I still do. I was able to overcome it by going to therapy and also by participating in sports. When I did well on the playing field it gave me confidence, and when you have confidence in yourself and feel good about yourself, then your problems don't seem as big."

Chris's hero was Mike Singletary, who played linebacker for his favorite team, the Chicago Bears. A lot of people thought Singletary was too small to be a good NFL player. A lot of people thought Chris was too small to be a linebacker, too. Little did they know he would end up at a position that required even more size—defensive tackle.

The South Side park where Chris played football (left) was far less exciting than Soldier's Field, where the Bears play.

School Days

Chris Zorich lived just a few blocks from his elementary school. Until he was old enough to walk there alone, his mother took him on the back of her bicycle.

Chris enjoyed school. Whenever he needed help, the teachers were glad to give it to him—all he had to do was ask. His favorite teacher was Miss Davis, who taught him in third grade. Chris liked her because she often played the piano for her class. When Chris came home each day, his mother would be waiting to ask him how his day had been. The two spent a lot of time together, reading stories and looking at Chris's comic book collection. From his mother, he learned that reading could take him away from the peeling paint and cracked plaster of their apartment and visit fantastic, faraway places.

Chris did just enough to get by when he got to Chicago Vocational High School. When

Chris in the fourth grade

his football coach told him he might be able to earn a college scholarship, however, Chris started getting more serious about his studies, and stopped slacking off. In his senior year he had to take trigonometry, English, and history on top of his regular courses. Whenever Chris thought about giving up, he remembered that a college education would be a ticket to a better life. And he knew his mother deserved it.

"If you do not know how to read, you will not be able to function in society. Think about it. You have to read things every day simply to find out where you are going. I *loved* to read when I was a kid. Life would have been unbearable if I had not learned how. My favorite book was called *The Giving Tree*, but I also used to read a lot of comics. I started collecting them when I was nine years old and now I have over 10,000!

"I wish I had spent more time with my schoolwork. After school, sometimes I wouldn't do my homework. Instead, I would go out and play. I wish I had those days back."

College

Chris hits Navy's quarterback and causes a fumble.

Years

When Chris Zorich arrived at Notre Dame, he felt as if he were in another world, a world with no gangs, no guns, and no despair. Everyone was there to learn and improve themselves. He had never imagined such a place existed, but here he was. And he loved it!

And Notre Dame loved Chris. He was a little too slow to play linebacker, so coach Lou Holtz moved him to nose tackle, where he lined up against the opposing team's center. In his first game, he had 10 tackles and got in on two quarterback sacks against the University of Michigan. Chris really came into his own during his junior and senior seasons. He was honored as an All-American both years. In 1990, he won the Lombardi Award as the nation's best lineman, and he was selected as College Lineman of the Year by the prestigious Touchdown Club in both 1989 and 1990.

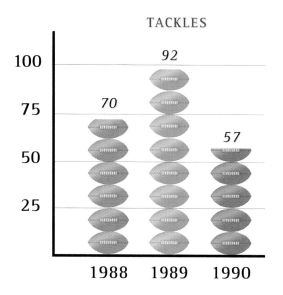

TACKLES

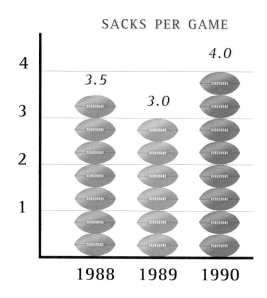

SACKS PER GAME

hris played his final game on New Year's Day, 1991. Notre Dame lost to Colorado in the Orange Bowl 10–9 and Chris was very sad. He called his mother, who told him she was very proud of his effort. That made Chris feel good. He said goodbye and I love you, and let her know he would be coming home tomorrow.

When Chris knocked on her door the next day, there was no answer. He knew immediately that something was wrong and broke into the apartment. Zora was lying on the floor. She had died of complications from her diabetes. Chris suddenly realized

Chris won the 1990 Vince Lombardi Award, given to the best college lineman.

that she would never enjoy the success he had worked so hard to achieve . . . and that, for the first time in his life, he would be alone. Chris decided to dedicate himself to making life better for people like his mother, whether he made it in the NFL or not.

"I wasn't even thinking about the pros, just about having a chance to play for Notre Dame, graduating in four years and getting a good-paying job so I could move my mom out of the neighborhood."

Chris became such a dominant player in the middle that Notre Dame's opponents actually stopped running the ball in his direction!

The Story

Although he was a great college player, some people thought Chris (left) was too short to play in the NFL.

Continues

Chris Zorich was drafted by the NFL team he had rooted for his entire life, the Chicago Bears. When he arrived in Bears training camp, many of the veteran players looked at the little defensive tackle and wondered how in the world he would survive in the NFL. Mike Singletary, however, could see that Chris would have no problem. Mike played linebacker and was Chicago's defensive captain. He was also Chris's childhood hero. Mike was at the end of a long, successful career. At the beginning of that career, no one thought he was big enough either. He and Chris knew that what you lack in size you can make up for by playing as hard as you can all the time.

Chris takes a break during his first practice as a professional football player.

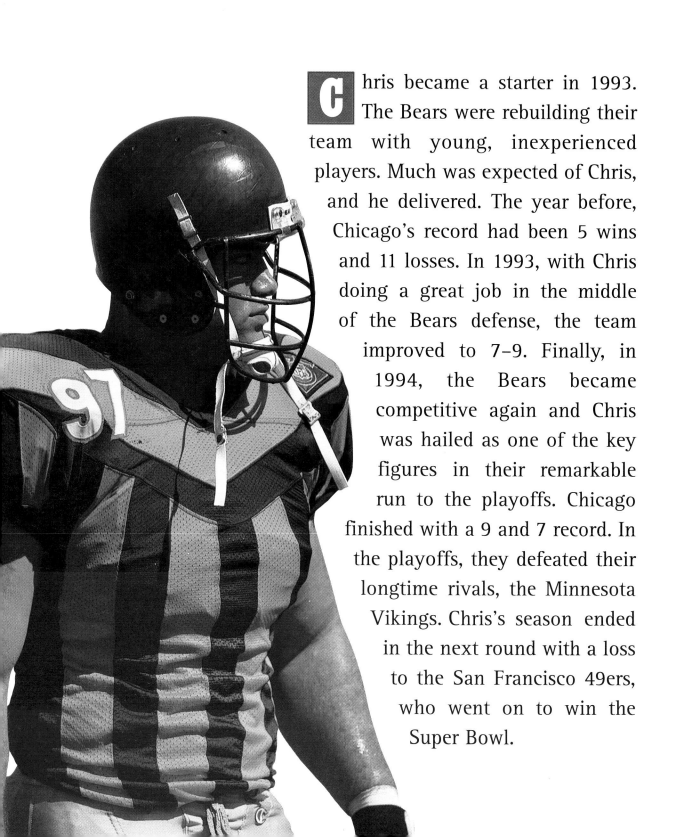

Chris became a starter in 1993. The Bears were rebuilding their team with young, inexperienced players. Much was expected of Chris, and he delivered. The year before, Chicago's record had been 5 wins and 11 losses. In 1993, with Chris doing a great job in the middle of the Bears defense, the team improved to 7–9. Finally, in 1994, the Bears became competitive again and Chris was hailed as one of the key figures in their remarkable run to the playoffs. Chicago finished with a 9 and 7 record. In the playoffs, they defeated their longtime rivals, the Minnesota Vikings. Chris's season ended in the next round with a loss to the San Francisco 49ers, who went on to win the Super Bowl.

Randall McDaniel (64)
and the Minnesota
Vikings could not
beat Chris's
Chicago Bears in
the 1994 playoffs.

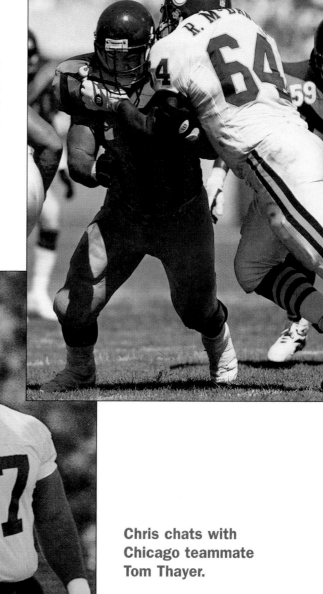

Chris chats with
Chicago teammate
Tom Thayer.

Timeline

1986: Leaves Chicago to attend Notre Dame University in South Bend, Indiana

1990: Leads Notre Dame to the national championship with a 34–21 win over West Virginia in the Fiesta Bowl

1991:
Drafted
by the
Chicago
Bears

1993:
Records
seven
quarterback
sacks during
the regular
season

1994: Helps
the Bears beat
the Vikings
35–18 in the
NFC playoffs

Game

Mike Singletary

In 1991 and 1992, Chris played on the same defensive squad as his idol, Mike Singletary (left).

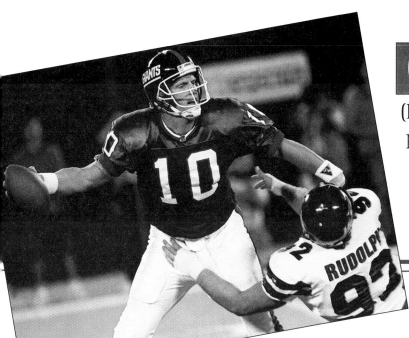

Chris's college roommate, quarterback Kent Graham (left), was drafted by the New York Giants in 1992. In 1995, Chris burned the Giants for two sacks and six solo tackles.

Action!

Chris's most thrilling moment in the NFL came against the Dallas Cowboys in the final game of the 1992 season. He recovered a fumble and ran into the end zone for a touchdown.

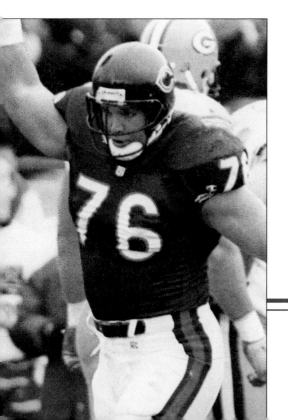

Chris got a chance to play with Steve McMichael (left) from 1991 to 1993. Like Chris, Steve played all-out all the time and became a star, even though he lacked the natural ability of other players.

Quick and aggressive, Chris loves to tackle quarterbacks. Here, he takes down Craig Erickson of Tampa Bay (left) and Neil O'Donnell of Pittsburgh (opposite page).

"My best game? I haven't had it yet. Not until I make every tackle!"

Dealing

Being one of the smallest players out there, I feel as though I am faster and can make a lot more plays than a lot of other guys."

I'm not going to grow anymore. What you see is what you get. If I make a play, I make a play. If I don't, I'm not going to blame it on not being tall enough."

With It

How Does

I t takes a monster to dominate the middle in the NFL. Chris Zorich is a "self-made" monster. Starting in high school—when he captained the power lifting team—right up until today, Chris has used weights to put 275 pounds of raw muscle on his 6 foot, 1 inch frame. He works out five times a week in order to keep up with the players who are paid to block him.

"I know there's a center out there who lifted today. Who's to say that one extra lifting day is not going to make him a little bit stronger in the fourth quarter . . . so he can kick my butt."

Ask NFL scouts if Chris is big enough to play his position and they will tell you flat-out: No. Ask the same scouts who they would most want on the field for a big play, and they will have to admit that Chris is right there at the top of the list. How does a player who is normally outweighed by 30 to 50 pounds keep from getting burned by blockers? By being quick off the

He Do It?

ball and literally running around the blocks! Chris has become an expert at recognizing which way a play is going and then darting past the center before he has a chance to set up. Once in a while Chris will get creamed—it happens to the best of them—but his combination of intelligence and speed make him every bit as dangerous as some of the 330-pounders who play his position.

The Grind

Chris helps a child lace on skates during "Skate on State," a charity skating event on Chicago's State Street.

Chris and friends join Disney characters on ice in "Skate on State."

C hris Zorich does not mind the demands of life in the NFL. Nothing was tougher than making it out of his old neighborhood alive. Still, being in the public eye can be very tiring sometimes, especially when you do as much off the field work as Chris does.

"The responsibility is the hardest thing about being a professional athlete. Whether you like it or not, you are a role model for children. I happen to like it."

Family

C hris Zorich remembers many Thanksgivings when he and his mother would wait for hours outside a local church to receive a holiday food basket. He knew his mom could not stand for more than a few minutes at a time without experiencing terrible pain, but she stood there suffering in silence so they could have something special to eat. In memory of his mother, Chris started a program to deliver groceries to more than 200

Matters

needy families—many of them in his old neighborhood. He also makes sure that all the mothers in a local shelter receive flowers on Mother's Day.

"Waiting in line as a little kid makes an impression on you. I swore that I'd never make anyone stand in line for food. I know that's what my mom would want me to do. I hope she's proud."

Chris's Uncle Lou is a professional actor who appeared on the TV series "Brooklyn Bridge." Lou is married to Olympia Dukakis, who won an Academy Award for her work in the movie *Moonstruck*.

Chris's Uncle Lou and his wife, Olympia Dukakis

Say What?

What do football people say about Chris Zorich?

"Chris never stops working when he's on the field."
—*Clarence Brooks,*
  Chris's defensive line coach

"He's scary."
—*Tommy Vardell,*
  Browns running back

"He has a burning desire to be the best."
—*Pat Haden, sportscaster*

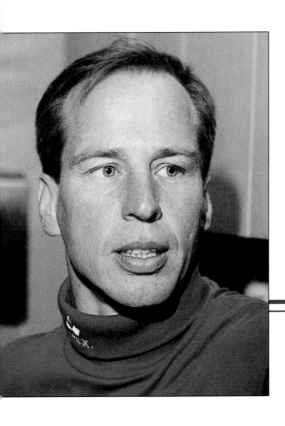

"He's big enough for us. And he shows up real big on Sundays . . . that's when it counts."

—*Bob Slowik,*
  Chris's defensive coach

"He attacks a problem the way he plays football. That's why he's a winner."

—*John Potocki, Chris's high-school coach*

"Zorich is too good, he's too dominant, he's too talented, he's too competitive to expect anyone to block him one-on-one."

—*Bill McCartney,*
  University of Colorado coach

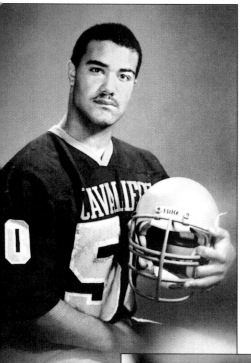

Career

Chris was an All-State linebacker at Chicago Vocational High School, following in the footsteps of CVHS defensive legends Dick Butkus and Keena Turner.

Chris was one of four Notre Dame players to gain All-America honors in 1990. Chris, Todd Lyght, Rocket Ismail, and Michael Stonebreaker all went on to play in the NFL.

Highlights

Chris could not believe his luck when Chicago selected him with the 49th pick of the 1991 NFL draft—he had been a huge Bears fan all of his life. Chris once said that he could not imagine playing for any other team. Chris led all Bears linemen in tackles in 1993 and 1994. He recorded a career-best seven quarterback sacks in 1993.

Reaching

Out

The Christopher Zorich Foundation takes kids to a local hockey game.

Chris does some of his finest work off the field, with the Chris Zorich Foundation. Through the foundation, he donates $97 (his uniform number) for each tackle he makes during the season, and challenges local companies to do the same. The money is channeled into a number of wonderful programs. Among Chris's favorites is the one where 15 kids get to attend a game as his guests . . . and then go out to dinner with him at Planet Hollywood. During the summer—when the Bears are not playing—he treats the kids to a day at Great America amusement park. The Zorich Foundation also awards a scholarship to Notre Dame in the name of Chris's mother.

Chris interviews the applicants, most of whom come from backgrounds similar to his own.

Chris signs a teddy bear Christmas present.

"I'm not saying I'm going to change the world . . . I just want to help others."

Numbers

Name: Christopher Robert Zorich
Born: May 13, 1969
Height: 6' 1"

Weight: 280 pounds
Uniform Number: 97
College: Notre Dame University

C hris says he chose number 97 out of respect for the great Dan Hampton, who had worn 99 for the Bears from 1979 to 1990. When Chris was offered 99, he did not feel he had earned the right to wear Hampton's number.

Season	Team	Games	Tackles	Sacks
1991	Chicago Bears	12	10	0.0
1992	Chicago Bears	16	53	2.0
1993	Chicago Bears	16	121	7.0
1994	Chicago Bears	16	104	5.5
1995	Chicago Bears	16	79	1.0
Totals		76	367	15.5

What If...

My quickness and anticipation enabled me to excel at football when a lot of people said I was too small. Notre Dame gave me a chance to play and prove myself, but the university also gave me a chance to learn. What if my critics had been right? What if I had lacked the skills to make up for my size disadvantage? Well, I still got a great education. I majored in American Studies, which exposed me to a lot of new ideas and inspiring people. And it gave me a clearer idea of what I could do with my life. I knew that if I didn't make it in the NFL, I could succeed in other ways. I think I would have started an orphanage. In fact, when my playing days are over, I may still do that."

Glossary

ABANDONED deserted; left alone

CHANNELED sent to different places

CONFIDENCE a feeling of trust and belief in oneself

CORSAGE a flower or tiny bouquet of flowers worn by a woman

CRITIC a person who finds fault with another's work, or who doubts another's abilities

DIABETES a disease in which there is too much sugar in the blood

DOMINANT the most powerful person or team

DOMINATE to rule with strength or power

FUNCTION the reason for using a person or object; use

LACKED needed a missing ingredient

LURK to hide close by, ready and waiting to appear

MAJOR the main subject of courses one studies in college; a math major takes mostly math

MENTAL having to do with the mind or thinking (rather than the physical body)

PRESTIGIOUS highly respected

RECRUITER one who tries to get people to join their team or organization

REQUIRED called for; necessary

SCHOLARSHIP money given to a student to help pay for schooling

SLACK OFF to be lazy or irresponsible

STUTTER a speech disorder in which one repeats sounds or words

TAUNT to tease or make fun of someone

THERAPY treatment for a mental or physical problem

VETERAN one who has a lot of experience

VOCATIONAL (HIGH SCHOOL) a school that trains students in a certain skill or trade to be used in a career

#

About The Author

Mark Stewart grew up in New York City in the 1960s and 1970s—when the Mets, Jets, and Knicks all had championship teams. As a child, Mark read everything about sports he could lay his hands on. Today, he is one of the busiest sportswriters around. Since 1990, he has written close to 500 sports stories for kids, including profiles on more than 200 athletes, past and present. A graduate of Duke University, Mark served as senior editor of *Racquet*, a national tennis magazine, and was managing editor of *Super News*, a sporting goods industry newspaper. He is the author of every Grolier All-Pro Biography.